AF256147

HISTORY
ON THE
HOMEFRONT

An American Tradition

100th Anniversary of the Service Flag

VOLUME 1

HISTORY
ON THE
HOMEFRONT

An American Tradition

100th Anniversary of the Service Flag

VOLUME 1

NICHOLAS D. SNIDER

with Pat Stansbury

PRESENTED BY THE NATIONAL FOUNDATION OF PATRIOTISM

Published by:
National Foundation of Patriotism
Buford, Georgia

ISBN: 978-1-7323427-2-9

Project Management: The Cadence Group
Photo Credit: Elizabeth Ordu and Nancy Tawes

CONTENTS

THE COLLECTION 13

PREFACE

When WWI Army Captain Robert L. Queisser of the Fifth Ohio Infantry, who had two sons serving on the front line, designed the original in-service flag, he quite possibly had no idea what a craze he was initiating. America loves her heroes and she-roes. So when someone comes up with the right idea at the right time and it brings us all together in a single voice, it takes on a life of its own and lives on throughout history. The following collection depicts the amazing ways people caught on and put their own spin on it. Patriotism in its finest hour!

STATEMENT BY MEDAL OF HONOR RECIPIENT
HERSHEL "WOODY" WILLIAMS,
last surviving Medal of Honor recipient of WWII Battle at Iwo Jima:

"It's important that we preserve our patriotic history in America for the next generation, and I think the National Foundation of Patriotism does a fine job in doing just that."

WELCOME FROM THE AUTHOR

I'd like to pull up a chair and say thank you for buying our book and helping support the National Foundation of Patriotism. As a collector, I had so much fun finding and preserving over ten thousand pieces of patriotic history. This book features the most exquisite, rare, and unique pieces on the subject of the in-service flag.

I must introduce you to Pat Stansbury. She is the EXECUTIVE DIRECTOR of the NATIONAL FOUNDATION OF PATRIOTISM, and we thank her for her ten years of devoted leadership. Her role here was to edit my longhand pages. She has also guided our outreach effort to reach nearly 375,000 people following us on social media. Her grasp of this subject and love for our followers are what made the enormous task of writing this book so enjoyable.

Whether you are a collector, a military supporter, a vintage jewelry lover, or the family member or friend of a veteran, there is something for you in this book. I have incorporated many rare treasures that might delight even the most die-hard collector of this genre. Moreover, I have included historic perspective and certain points of interest you won't want to miss. We wrote a book, not a catalogue. A book about love, war, history, and patriotism. This book doesn't tell you to be a patriot; we hope it will inspire you to be one. To care about our soldiers and their families. To care about love and peace on the home front. To act on what you feel and share what you learn.

Patriotism is the DNA of America; it's what keeps this country together. I like to ask people, "Are we finished building America?" Most people give me a resounding NO!

As I write my closing comments, I want to invite each of you to carefully consider your role in building a better, stronger, and safer America. These words are not new or unique, but they are meaningful.

So here's my call to action!

1. Display an in-service flag or banner in your window if you have a family member serving in the US Armed Forces. (We have included one you can cut out in this book.)

2. Display an American flag above it (always in the place of highest honor).

3. Celebrate patriotic holidays with your family and tell them why it's important to you.

4. Please support the National Foundation of Patriotism. Help us keep patriotism alive!

5. Buy copies of this book as gifts and help us teach the next generation the importance of patriotism and collecting. Make *History on the Home Front* your American tradition!

Thank you,

Nick

FROM THE DESK OF THE EXECUTIVE DIRECTOR

The first time I met Nick Snider, I was introduced to his sweetheart jewelry collection. I found it so fascinating that someone would preserve this piece of romantic history.

Without the stories to go with the pieces, people may gloss right over it and never actually appreciate the value of this historic perspective on love, war, and patriotism.

I became an instant volunteer at his National Museum of Patriotism and later was promoted to executive director. It is a sincere honor to assist him in writing this book after ten years of promoting and presenting this collection to thousands of visitors in Atlanta, as well as through our traveling exhibits elsewhere.

Now that we converted the National Museum of Patriotism to a virtual museum online called the National Foundation of Patriotism, we are reaching almost a half million people through social media.

On a personal level, I am the sister of a 100 percent disabled Vietnam veteran and the mother of a West Point combat experienced officer. I am happy to report both men are doing well at this time. I was sincerely humbled at the opportunity to work for the National Museum of Patriotism during my son's years of service. My work afforded me the ability to promote patriotism nationwide in an effort to be sure my son would come home to a more grateful America in 2012 than my brother did in 1967.

This exhibit speaks to military families and "military-friendly" families across America who understand that a strong, patriotic America leads to a safer global community. Patriotism strengthens the bonds of peace in our society. We must do our part in encouraging those around us to see the value and the benefit of living peacefully and creating strong, supportive communities.

This exhibit is only part of Nick's entire collection. But it is a very important piece of American history that we might have missed had he not continued collecting for over forty years.

The ground beneath the American flag is level, and I encourage every American to show their patriotism by displaying the flag freely.

Patriotism: it's all about peace; it's all about love; it's all about unity.

Pat Stansbury

ACKNOWLEDGMENTS

It is with a truly grateful heart that I write the acknowledgments to this book. I've been collecting for over forty years and have met an enormous number of people. I wish I had the memory to name each and every one of them from over thirty states and five countries. I will do my best to acknowledge those who had a hand in bringing this book to market.

I would be remiss if I did not pay tribute to my executive director, Pat Stansbury. For over ten years she has offered her insight, moral support, leadership, and intuition to all the many projects I have undertaken. She took this collection with all the rust and dust it came with and oversaw the production of this book and the life of the physical collection and its preservation and outreach. She also edited the mountains of pages I wrote longhand and made them into a concise, readable, historically accurate (to the best of our ability) document.

Our publishing consultant at The Cadence Group; GKS Creative, for graphic design; and photographers Nancy Tawes of Nancy Tawes Photography and Elizabeth Ordu of Elizabeth O Photography.

I hope you will enjoy this book as more of a fireside chat than a catalog of relics.

My family is my treasure. I thank them for the unwavering support and encouragement they have afforded throughout my adult life.

My family:

Chris Snider and Siobhan Tinsley	Tim Snider
Susan and Scott McDowell	Warren Snider
Roger and Sherry Snider	

A special appreciation for my fellow collectors and authors, who have inspired me to keep seeking adventure:

Ron and Kate Wallace	Hershel and Jody Khan
Arthur and Joyce Johnston	Art Johnston
Steve and Leslie Walden	

It's been said, "No man is a failure if he has friends!" That makes me especially blessed to have so many.

A grateful thanks to a partner in patriotism who keeps our collection on public display at the Hartsfield-Jackson International Airport:

David Vogt (HJIA Art Director)

And to my fellow collectors:

Larry and Denise Baker	Pat Boarders
Ron Burkey	Joe and Denise Groseclose
Woody Heath	Pat Jacob
Walter and Merle Koester	Patricia Koester-Smith
Jan and Chris Long	Earl Reed
Randy and Cecilia Sheffield	Tony and Linda Wimmer

THE HEART OF A COLLECTOR: WHY WE COLLECT

Why do we collect? During my research for this book, I found there are about as many theories on the subject as there are things to collect. It became such a bizarre study; I just have to share my favorites before giving my personal views. Here we go!

One psychoanalytical view is that unloved children seek personal comfort in accumulating things.

Another psychoanalyst cited collecting as motivated by existential anxieties. The collection in and of itself is an extension of our identity and actually lives on long after we are gone.

How about this one? Some evolutionary theorists support the idea that somehow when humans create a collection, it's actually their way of attracting potential mates, thus showcasing their ability to accumulate resources.

How about the endowment effect? This is a phenomenon that subscribes to the idea that some people have a tendency to value things more once they actually possess them themselves.

It gets better! How about the concept of contagion? Supposedly some collectors are attracted to other people's belongings, such as those of celebrities, because these objects are believed to be infused with the essence of the person who previously owned them.

According to Christian Jarrett, a psychologist and author:

"Humans are unique in the way we collect items purely for the satisfaction of seeking and owning them. The desire to collect only became possible about 12,000 years ago, once our ancestors gave up their nomadic lifestyles and settled down in one location."

Carl Jung, a Swiss psychiatrist and psychoanalyst, theorized this:

He touted the influence of the concept of archetypes on behavior, meaning there are certain universal symbols that are embedded in our "collective unconscious." Therefore, completing sets, as in collecting, compels us to relate to our archetypical antecedents in gathering berries, nuts, and things needed for survival by our alleged earlier ancestors.

However, and not surprising to some, Sigmund Freud must be included in the collective voice on why we collect. According to Freud, collecting stems from our potty training days, citing our sense of loss of control of our own bodies. Therefore, collectors are trying to gain back control by "possessing" that which was lost to us so long ago. You might say that Sigmund's conclusion is that collecting is a delayed response to literally pissing away our sense of control! (Sorry, I just couldn't resist.)

I, on the other hand, was never quite that complex in my ideology. Basically, I collect things I like, and I enjoy the historic value of the pieces. My desire has always been to share them with others, thereby imparting information, historic perspective, and good old "look what I found" fun.

Collecting has been a very fulfilling part of my life. The total experience is my passion. It's meeting the sellers, fellow collectors, and inheritors who want to pass on the beloved items left to them so that the items may circulate beyond a box in the attic.

The joy of rummaging through rust and dust to find these tiny treasures has always yielded a surge of adrenaline to which only true collectors can relate. It gets inside you and drives you to keep searching. And true collectors never see a finish line.

My collection has taken on quite an illustrious life! It has been housed in my museum from 1996 to 2010, the National Museum of Patriotism, and has been on loan to many museums, corporate offices, government offices, and colleges on an ongoing basis. *Antiques Roadshow* was hosted at the museum in 2006, and *CBS News Sunday Morning* actually visited the collection in a warehouse while it was in transit, before finding its way to broader and larger displays. Since 2008 a small representation of my collection is featured in a display case at Hartsfield-Jackson International Airport in Atlanta. We are currently working with longtime friend and airport art director, David Vogt, on an expansion of a new display case due to be unveiled in late 2020–2021.

In conclusion, I will share about my conversation with the Smithsonian Institution's officials, who happily accepted my collection for the preservation of its historic value. However, I learned that my collection, albeit "preserved," would probably never reach the wide eyes of its viewers, as it would be contained in one of about four hundred warehouses. This made my collector's heart sink. I'd rather put them in cigar boxes and bury them all around the country and start a nationwide treasure hunt! Now THAT is a good idea! Maybe my descendants will one day be interested in that kind of hoopla. For now, I need to finish writing this book.

THE COLLECTOR'S EXPERIENCE

Let me take a moment and share some thoughts with you about how I feel when describing each one of these collectibles. It's not easy to make descriptions very editorially interesting. The challenge is in the repetition necessary for accuracy, along with the excitement I feel about having found each treasured piece.

Collecting, as in most everything, has its exciting moments, its frustrating moments, as well as its downright boring moments as you scan and scour for pieces you thought you saw a few minutes prior and now cannot for the life of you find!

It's what you sense when you take your first step into a military show—the grit on the hard concrete underfoot, the stagnant air of a cavernous convention center filled with old relics (human as well as material)—and catch the first sight of a familiar face from last year's show that your heart starts pumping. It's the rhythm of anticipation and excitement. Maybe he has something new this year. You offer to help him get set up just so you can get a peek before the vultures land.

The thrill of the find and the agony of the shutout! At the end of the show, you're still feeling like a winner as you carry your bag to the car.

At this point, I'm anxious to get back to my hotel room to conduct my own one-man "show and tell." This truly becomes the highlight of the day. It gives me outstanding pleasure to see the great history I rescued and the anticipation of sharing it with others.

A glance over my shoulder as I back out of my parking space gives rise to the excitement of already looking forward to next year's show!

A MILITARY MOTHER'S PERSPECTIVE ON LOVE, WAR, AND PATRIOTISM

One West Point Mom's Story of Life, Love, Deployment, and Patriotism

I have never felt so alone in my life. Having recently gotten divorced after almost thirty years of marriage, it was surreal to stand there without my husband as our first son graduated from West Point. There I stood looking out on the Hudson River, full of pride, fear, and a mix of other emotions I would come to terms with in time. He was about to fulfill his commitment to duty, honor, and country when an icy breeze seemed to brush across my shoulders.

As he took his oath, I remembered teaching this little boy as he so diligently tried to learn the Pledge of Allegiance. I remembered teaching him to pray and to honor God in all he thought, did, and said. I remembered teaching him how the God of the universe formed him in the palm of His hand, in His own image, and had a magnificent plan for his life. And that we must pray every day to learn that mission and be prepared when we find it. We also prayed for the little girl, wherever she was, whom God chose to be his wife.

Before I knew it, he was running across the lawn one day, waving a letter over his head. He was commissioned to attend the United States Military Academy at West Point. The painfully difficult and lonely years at the academy were softened one night not long before graduation by a call home: "Mom, I met a girl." I knew that tone; I was cautiously delighted.

No matter how alone I felt that day, I was accompanied by my other three children, my sister, her husband, our adopted Gramma Rose, and Maria. God's plan unfolded while we watched his brother pin him, shake hands, and embrace.

So here I was, on that bank of the Hudson River, facing the Mission, standing with The Girl. The girl who would take my son's hand and wait with me for the next five years through every deployment and every return.

The first deployment was so hard, I thought I'd die as I felt his hand slip from mine in a final farewell before he left. I'll never forget how he smiled back at me over his shoulder, walking away from me. That hand that just slipped from mine was the grown-up "man hand" of the little boy whom I'd held in my arms and protect him from harm, fear, and sadness. The same hands I kissed when he fell down, or held when we walked, or high-fived when we celebrated. That same precious hand now embraces a weapon and a Bible. Those hands will serve him in combat and compassion.

November 7, 2008, he returned safely home. November 7, 2009, we were preparing for deployment once again. This time, Maria and I were joined by three-month-old Sophia, whom God created to fill our arms as he emptied our hearts once again.

My prayer for all military families is that you'll stand with us in the following disciplines in honor of our soldiers and our country:

- Stay close as a family. And reach out to other military families in tangible ways.
- Stay close to God. Allow His Almighty Hand to guide your soldier and comfort you while you wait those endless hours; you are not alone.
- Stay patriotic. We owe it to our veterans, who paid the price for the freedoms we are enjoying right now: freedom of speech, freedom from want, freedom from fear, freedom of religion, and freedom of choice. And we owe it to the next generation to preserve those freedoms by protecting the respect of our US Constitution.

God bless you, God bless your soldier, and God bless America.

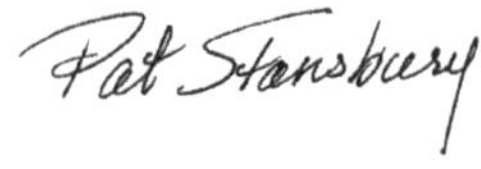

HISTORY OF THE IN-SERVICE FLAG

The history and origin of the service flag is as heartwarming as the subject it represents. It's a symbol of patriotism and pride to each family who displays it. It is officially defined as a white field with a red border and a blue star for each family member serving in the United States Armed Forces during any period of war or hostilities in which we are engaged. A gold star will cover the blue star, representing the service member has died.

The original in-service flag was designed to be an indoor wartime flag, generally about a foot long and usually suspended vertically from a cord in a window for public view. A stick was often sewn onto the top of the flag with a cord or string attached at both ends.

The flag was designed and patented by Captain Robert L. Queisser, serving during World War I in the Fifth Ohio Infantry. He had two sons serving on the front line. He wanted to remind the nation of the sacrifice and heroism of our servicemen and women during their tour of duty. The Queisser flag launched a nationwide surge of patriotic pride among families that soon inspired businesses and churches as well.

Early flags were handmade by military mothers, wives, or sweethearts during World War I. They were made of wool at first and later cotton bunting during World War II. Finally, mass production yielded in-service flags from other materials as well, such as felt or satin.

Churches and businesses displayed larger flags in order to accommodate the larger number of members or employees on active duty. Blue stars would be covered or replaced with a gold star in the event that a member had died.

THE PATRIOTIC PROGRESSION
OF THE IN-SERVICE FLAGS AND BANNERS

Based upon its original design, patented in 1917, the in-service flag became the unofficial symbol of a son or husband in service; that is, until President Woodrow Wilson and the Woman's Committee of the Council of National Defense became part of its history in 1918. Their influence and support fueled the flames of patriotic fervor—which, quite frankly, was waning as our nation contemplated our role in the world beyond our borders.

In 1942 the Blue Star Mothers of America was founded as a veteran service organization. They became part of the movement to provide care packages to military members serving overseas and assistance to the families who encountered hardship as a result of a husband or son serving during combat. The practice of the display of the service flag gained momentum and became more widespread. Soon, it seemed virtually every home and organization had an in-service flag on display.

The number of stars on the flag indicated the number of members of the family or organization serving in the Armed Forces at the time. Sadly, the fact that blue stars became covered with gold stars at homes, businesses, and churches preserved the magnitude of the sacrifice so many families endured. This drove home the desire to honor the memory of our servicemen and women.

HISTORY OF THE *IN FLANDERS FIELDS* POEM

McCrae's *In Flanders Fields* remains to this day one of the most memorable war poems ever written.

It is the lasting legacy of the terrible battle in the Ypres Salient continuing in the spring 1915. Here is the story of the making of that poem:

Although he had been a doctor for many years and had served in the South African War, it was impossible to get used to the suffering, the screams, and the blood here, and Major John McCrae had seen and heard enough in his dressing station to last a lifetime.

As a surgeon attached to the first field artillery brigade, Major McCrae, who had joined the McGill faculty in 1900 after graduating from the University of Toronto, had spent seventeen days treating injured men—Canadians, British, Indians, French, and Germans—in the Ypres Salient.

It had been an ordeal he had hardly thought possible. McCrae later wrote of it: "I wish I could embody on paper some of the varied sensations of that 17 days . . . 17 days of Hades! At the end of the first day, if anyone had told us we had to spend 17 days there, we would have folded our hands and said it could not have been done."

One death particularly affected McCrae. A young friend and former student, Lt. Alexis Helmer of Ottawa, had been killed by a shell burst on 2 May 1915. Lieutenant Helmer was buried later that day in the little cemetery outside McCrae's dressing station, and McCrae had performed the funeral ceremony in the absence of the chaplain.

The next day, sitting on the back of an ambulance parked by the dressing station beside the Canal de l'Yser, just a few hundred yards north of Ypres, McCrae vented his anguish by composing a poem. The major was no stranger to writing, having authored several medical texts and dabbled in poetry.

In the nearby cemetery McCrae could see the wild poppies that sprang up in the ditches in that part of Europe, and he spent twenty minutes of precious rest time scribbling fifteen lines of verse in a notebook.

A young soldier watched him write it. Cyril Allinson, a twenty-two-year-old sergeant major, was delivering mail that day when he spotted McCrae. The major looked up as Allinson approached then went on writing while the sergeant major stood there quietly. "His face was very tired but calm as he wrote," Allinson recalled. "He looked around from time to time, his eyes straying to Helmer's grave."

When McCrae finished five minutes later, he took his mail from Allinson and without saying a word handed his pad to the young NCO. Allinson was moved by what he read: "The poem was an exact description of the scene in front of both of us. He used the word 'blow' in that line because the poppies were being blown that morning by a gentle east wind. It never occurred to me at that time that it would ever be published. It seemed to me an exact description of the scene."

In fact, it was very nearly not published. Dissatisfied with it, McCrae tossed the poem away, but a fellow officer retrieved it and sent it to news offices in England. *The Spectator*, in London, rejected it, but *Punch* published it on 8 December 1915.

In Flanders fields the poppies blow
Between the crosses, row on row,
That mark our place; and in the sky
The larks, still bravely singing, fly
Scarce heard amid the guns below.

We are the Dead. Short days ago
We lived, felt dawn, saw sunset glow,
Loved and were loved, and now we lie,
In Flanders fields.

Take up our quarrel with the foe:
To you from failing hands we throw
The torch; be yours to hold it high.
If ye break faith with us who die
We shall not sleep, though poppies grow
In Flanders fields.

Lieutenant Colonel John McCrae, MD (1872–1918), Canadian Army

THE OFFICIAL DISPLAY OF THE IN-SERVICE FLAG

In our society, we are seeing a tremendous swing of disrespect toward the American flag, the Pledge of Allegiance, and the National Anthem. Basically, patriotism is on the rails!

The good news is that, by and large, the country is very patriotic, law abiding, and peace loving. Still, we must do our part in honoring our American values by always treating people and patriotism with dignity and respect. We must handle, display, and wear the in-service flag properly as per the rules set forth by our government in keeping with propriety and the spirit of patriotic fervor.

If you pay careful consideration to the many ways the in-service flag has been used, you will also notice that these rules have historically been ignored. But we at the National Foundation of Patriotism give a respectful pass at this oversight due to its higher achievement in reuniting a nation at war.

So here they are, the United States Department of Defense directives on displaying and wearing the in-service flag:

- The service flag shall be treated with dignity and respect. When displayed with the flag of the United States, the service flag shall be of approximately equal size but never larger than the flag of the United States. The flag of the United States will occupy the position of honor.

- When the service flag is displayed other than by being flown from a staff, it will be suspended either horizontally or vertically.

- Users are cautioned against the use of the service flag for advertising purposes. It will not be embroidered on such articles as cushions, handkerchiefs, and the like; printed, or otherwise impressed on paper napkins or boxes or anything that is designed for temporary use and discarded; or used as any portion of a costume or athletic uniform. Advertising signs will not be fastened to a staff or halyard from which the service flag is flown.

- For cautions against the improper use of the service flag, users should be guided generally by the provisions of 36 U.S.C. 176, which apply to the flag of the United States of America.

THE COLLECTION

IN-SERVICE BANNERS/PENNANTS/FLAGS

The original in-service flag Captain Queisser designed was later imposed on all sorts of items that spoke to the pride and patriotism of the families who displayed them.

From 1917 to 1919 creative family members, mostly women, pooled their sewing talents to craft some of the most unique emblems to display their patriotic pride. They began to sew the in-service flag on items made of felt, cotton, and wool. In this banner exhibit, I

have many pieces that represent many different factions within the Armed Forces.

I have a few special and rare pieces. One I particularly favor is a double flag representing one son in the Signal Corps and the other son in the Aviation. I imagine they hung it with some sort of rotating hanger so you could see both sides. My second favorite, and the only one of its kind I've ever seen, is one that you hang on a door handle. It represents a soldier in the Engineer Corps. It states Engineer on top and the in-service flag in the middle, with the triple fortress towers under the flag. The maker realized that this special piece was one way to actually feel an item in the hand every time they entered through that door.

In viewing the banners in this collection, you can see the integrity of the banners has been carefully protected. Mostly made from wool, you can also see the tiny pinholes probably made by insects over time. I have compiled the best of my collection in this category, but I suspect there are still many more out there to discover. I say this to invite future collectors to join us!

Serious collectors will monitor eBay auctions and estate sales, as well as military shows, for maximum coverage during the search. Good luck on getting a good price!

The banners and pennants represented here are made from felt. There are three very unique pieces mentioned, which I will value here:

- Door hanger—one of a kind.
- Double-hung banner—one of a kind.
- Cavalry—rare.

Banners/Pennants WWI

The groups of banners illustrated here represent either the military branch or a section of the military branch. An example would be a banner with two large towers along a smaller tower in the middle, which signified that it was the Engineers section of the US Army.

You will see the Medical Corps identified with the medusa and the Artillery Corps identified with crossed cannons. The Signal Corps is identified with colored crossed flags and a torch in the center. The crossed sabers (swords) represents the US Army Cavalry. The standing eagle over the wheel with saber and key represent the quartermaster. A bomb with a fuse represents Ordnance. The machine gun represents the machine gun squad in a platoon or company. All banners are WWI.

Banners/Pennants Infantry

Banners/Pennants Quartermaster

"Because Duty Calls" is the motto of the American quartermaster. His or her job is to manage the day-to-day needs and living quarters of our servicemen and women.

Here are four examples of the uniformity of the in-service flag sewn onto varying shapes and sizes of felt banners and pennants.

Banners/Pennants Artillery

Banners/Pennants Ordnance

Banners/Pennants Medical

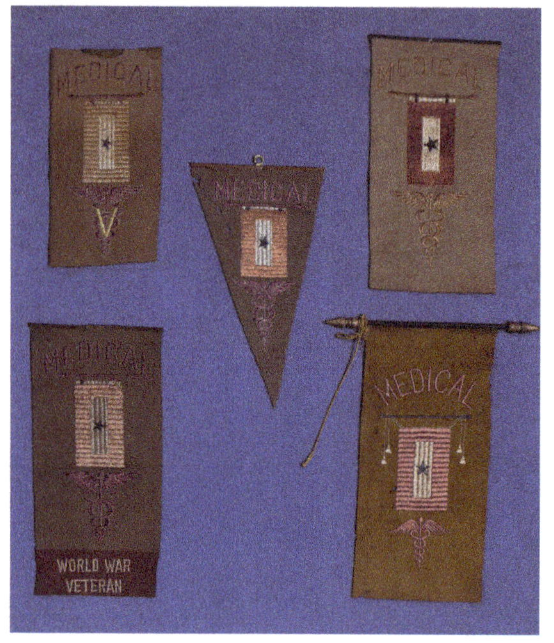

Banners/Pennants Hospital Corps

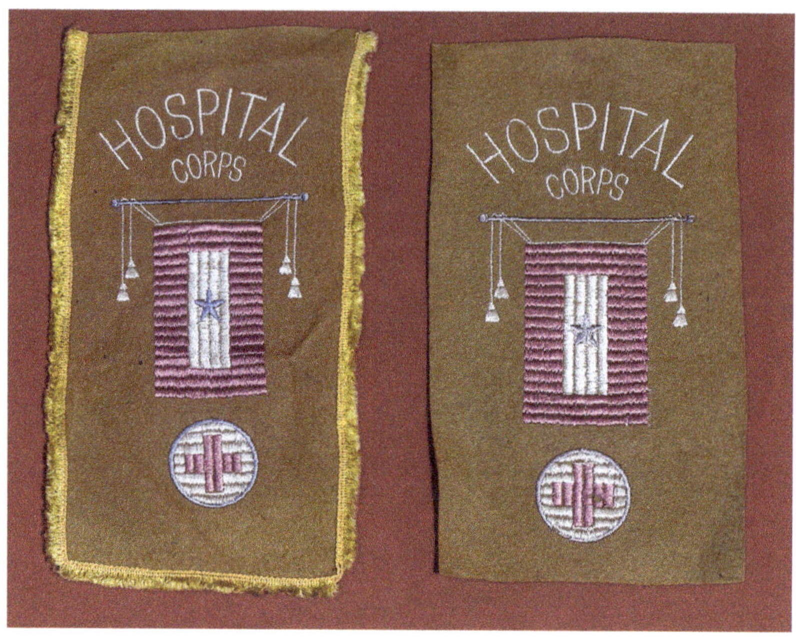

Banners/Pennants Aviation

Banners/Pennants Signal Corps

Banners/Pennants Engineers

Banners/Pennants Assorted

Banners/Pennants Machine Gun

Single Star In-Service Flags

Two-Star In-Service Flags

Three-Star In-Service Flags

Four-Star In-Service Flags

Five-Star In-Service Flags

In-Service Various Banners

When WWI Army Captain Robert L. Queisser of the Fifth Ohio Infantry, who had two sons serving on the front line, designed the original in-service flag, he quite possibly had no idea what a craze he was initiating. America loves her heroes and she-roes. So when someone comes up with the right idea at the right time, and it brings us all together in a single voice, it takes on a life of its own and lives on throughout history. The following collection depicts the amazing ways people caught on and put their own spin on it. Patriotism in its finest hour!

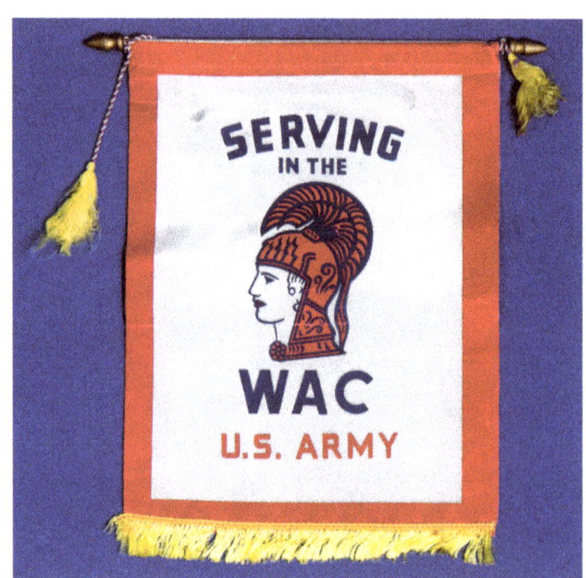

In-Service Very Unique Banners

These banners are unique in that they do not necessarily have any designation for a particular branch of service but they do have the emblem of a discharge lapel pin.

The rendering is intended to look like the American eagle, which is the common visual representation of America, commonly and affectionately referred to by military personal as the "ruptured duck."

The first banner (top left) depicts two eagles and a star, representing two family members honorably discharged and one still in service.

The second banner (bottom left): Honorably Discharged! This proud family wants the world to know their soldier is home. It's hard to choose which of the many banners in this selection is the most unusual, but this one ranks right up there.

The remaining banners are self-explanatory in that they convey clear messages of their intent.

This concludes the smaller window-sized banners meant to be displayed at home. I have taken great care to secure this unique and important piece of American history. Considering we had about five million men and women serve in WWI and around twenty million serve in WWII, this history on the home front touches the lives of most American citizens living today.

Vintage Photo In-Service Banners

This wonderful exhibit brings the entire collection to a whole new level of respect. You are now looking into the faces of some of the brave men who fought for your freedom! Hauntingly beautiful. I find it hard to look away from these photos.

The two happy fellows, possibly brothers, immortalized in this banner remind us of the sacrifice some families make with more than one soldier in service at a time.

(Incidentally, in my family, three brothers, a sister, and I all served in the United States Army. Although none of us served in combat, we were on active duty during WWII and the Korea and Vietnam Wars. Obviously we each served in our own era. During WWII our mother worked in the defense plant and a nephew served as an interpreter.)

This is a very unusual banner—a very proud family doing their patriotic duty at home. This lovely woman and her three children apparently anxiously waited for her husband to return home safely. Someone took great pride in preserving this family's dedication to America.

This obviously active duty military policeman has such a look of pride and victory in his eyes. It makes you proud to know that behind all the flag waving and parades we attend today are important reminders of the diligent work and risk our servicemen and women still commit to today for our safety and freedom!

This emblem is honoring a black sailor with the words "LET FREEDOM RING" and "GOD BLESS AMERICA" inscribed above and below him. Wouldn't it be wonderful to find the family this well-preserved banner belonged to?

WWI vintage felt photo pennant features a soldier proudly posing for his picture. Carefully placed in a fabric frame, mounted on this felt pennant above his in-service star and USA in vertical letters at the bottom. Fine craftsmanship and a wonderful reminder of the flesh and blood that is our Armed Forces.

Obviously the same crafter or manufacturer made this pennant for this soldier from Camp Lee, which tells us these were made in Virginia. The fine young men in these two pennants had parents and grandparents alive during the Civil War. That terrible war, where in some cases brothers fought brothers, reminds us how fragile and precious unifying the nation truly is. God blessed us through their service, and may God continue to bless America.

In-Service Interesting Group of Three Similar Banners

This group of three in-service banners is manufactured, which means they had to be ordered and specified. I believe they may have actually come from the same family, as the third and most-worn shows one member in service. This is the only time I've found three identical banners in which each respective piece adds one member in service, and the wear on the felt and embroidery as well as the fringe suggests an aging progression.

Honor Your American Heroes

This commercial banner, most commonly sold in big box stores, is one of four designs that represent military, fire, police, and general USA patriotism. The manufacturer states: "Military Service Flag, displaying this flag in your window honors your family members in the armed forces who are willing to give their lives to keep our country safe and free." Although this is a newly manufactured piece, it will be a collectible in the future!

In-Service Large Flags

This is the culmination of the banners and flags exhibit. If bigger is better, then this is best! Although it's difficult to give scale to each one of these in this selection, you can appreciate the heart of this enormous task. I attribute the Blue Star Mothers organization to the success of the in-service flag gaining momentum nationwide and in so doing, spreading and growing patriotic pride across America.

The in-service banner had humble beginnings as individual families honored their husbands and sons serving in the US Armed Forces. Once the Blue Star Mothers got ahold of it, they encouraged organizations to take part and drove their cause from Main Street to Wall Street! Soon, small businesses, churches, and later, large corporations joined in honoring the servicemen and women in their organizations. So the small, window-sized banner representing one service member grew to include the corporate employers creating gigantic flags with a star representing each of their employees currently serving in the war effort.

It bears mentioning that the largest and most amazing flag I've ever seen a picture of but I do not possess in my collection is the Marshall Field's flag! Weighing in at 500 pounds, 2,400 square feet, it recognizes 2,179 employees, each represented by one blue star. It's the only one to my knowledge that recognized the sixty-one women serving, as well; their stars are prominently placed in the center of the flag. There are also seven gold stars represented in this photo at the time of its shooting, June 26, 1943, which was about the midpoint of the war.

As you can see, the first is the largest flag in my collection. I'll start with this one for the purpose of giving scale to the rest. I stand five feet nine; each one thereafter is progressively smaller.

104,313
MINNESOTA
1,223

In-Service China-Burma-India Collection

During WWII the Japanese invaded the lower part of China and moved across Burma into India. The Allies—United States of America, Britain, China, and the Soviet Union—knew they must start an additional front to stop the advancement of the Japanese, and both Britain and the United States collaborated regarding how to fight back. The birth of the famed Flying Tigers was born under the masterful guidance of Colonel Chennault; his flyers were fearless. These men were charged with some of the most difficult battles in history of WWII.

There are many fine books that detail the heroics displayed by the Allied Forces in that engagement. The items that relate to our subject, in-service, depict the extreme nature of battle-weary warriors who retain tenderhearted sentiment toward their loved ones, particularly their sweethearts.

The China National Aviation Corps

The Chinese Air Force created this pin in 1929. During WWII, American Flying Tigers supported the Chinese Air Force in the China-Burma-India Campaign.

China-Burma-India Bracelets and Rings

As you study these beautifully crafted pieces, be sure to take note of these bracelets. One bracelet is inscribed with the words: "ELLA CORLES, PILOT'S WIFE." The underside of the bracelet is engraved: "Hands Off! She's mine. Capt. J. W. Corlis." This is a great example of the love of a husband for his wife back home.

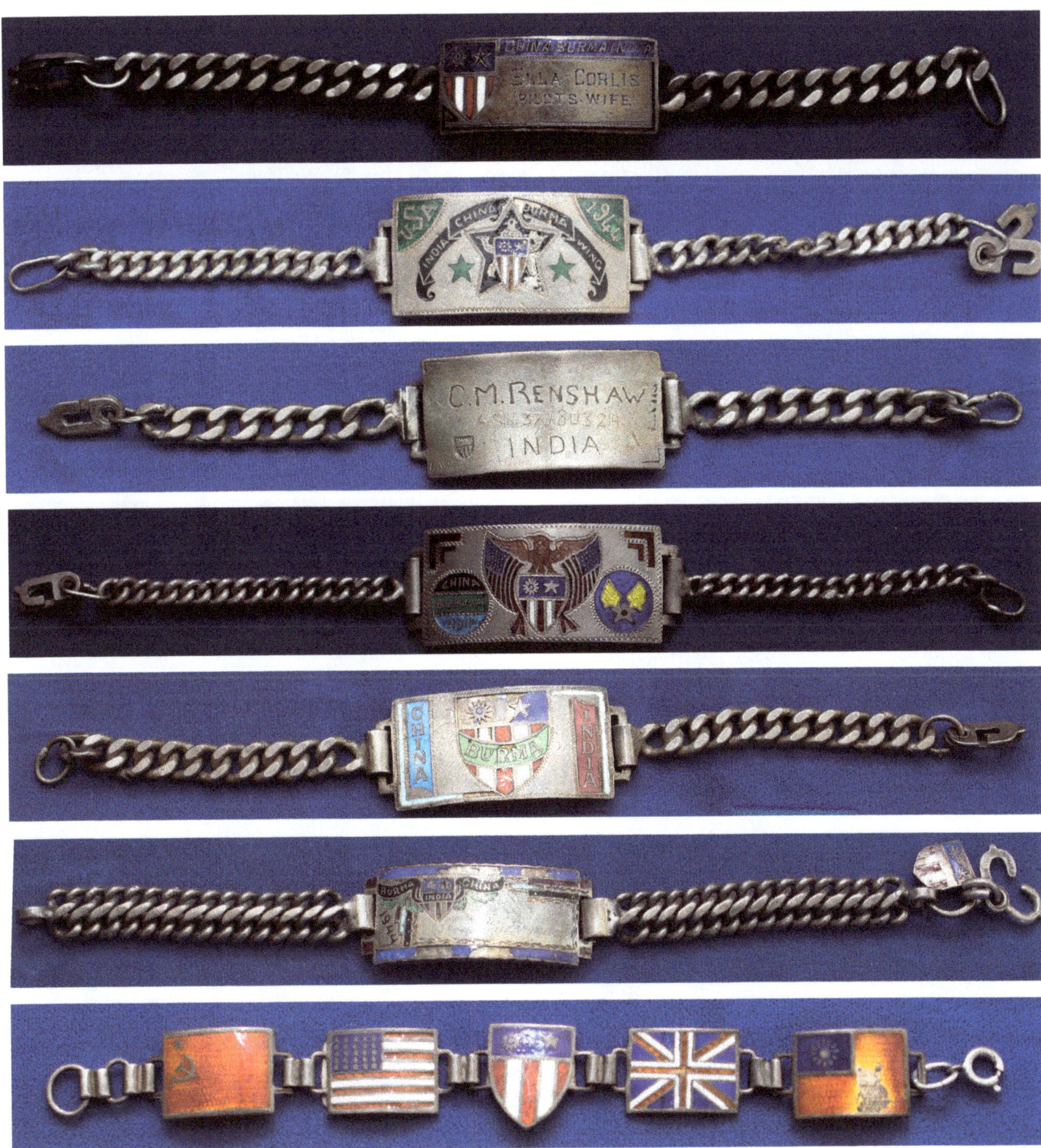

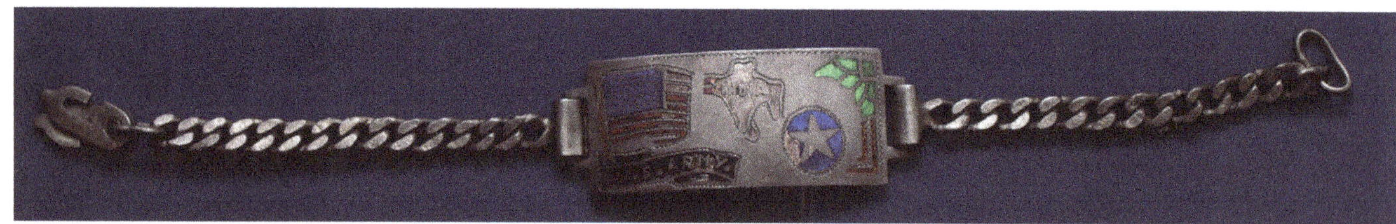

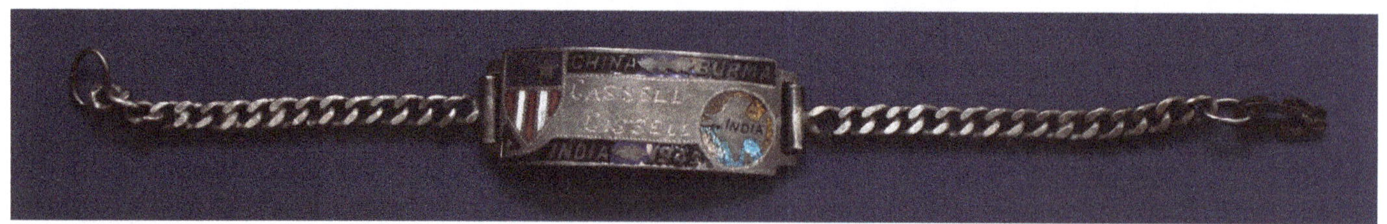

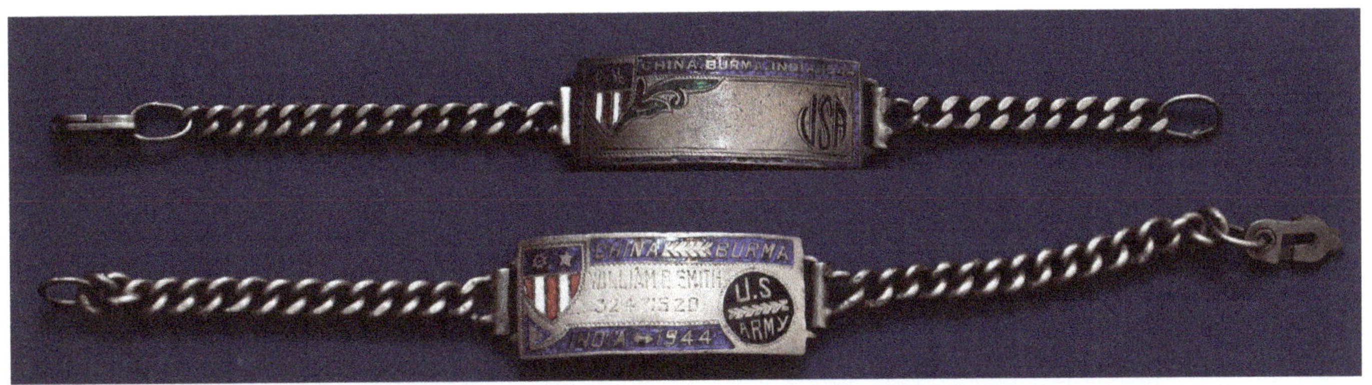

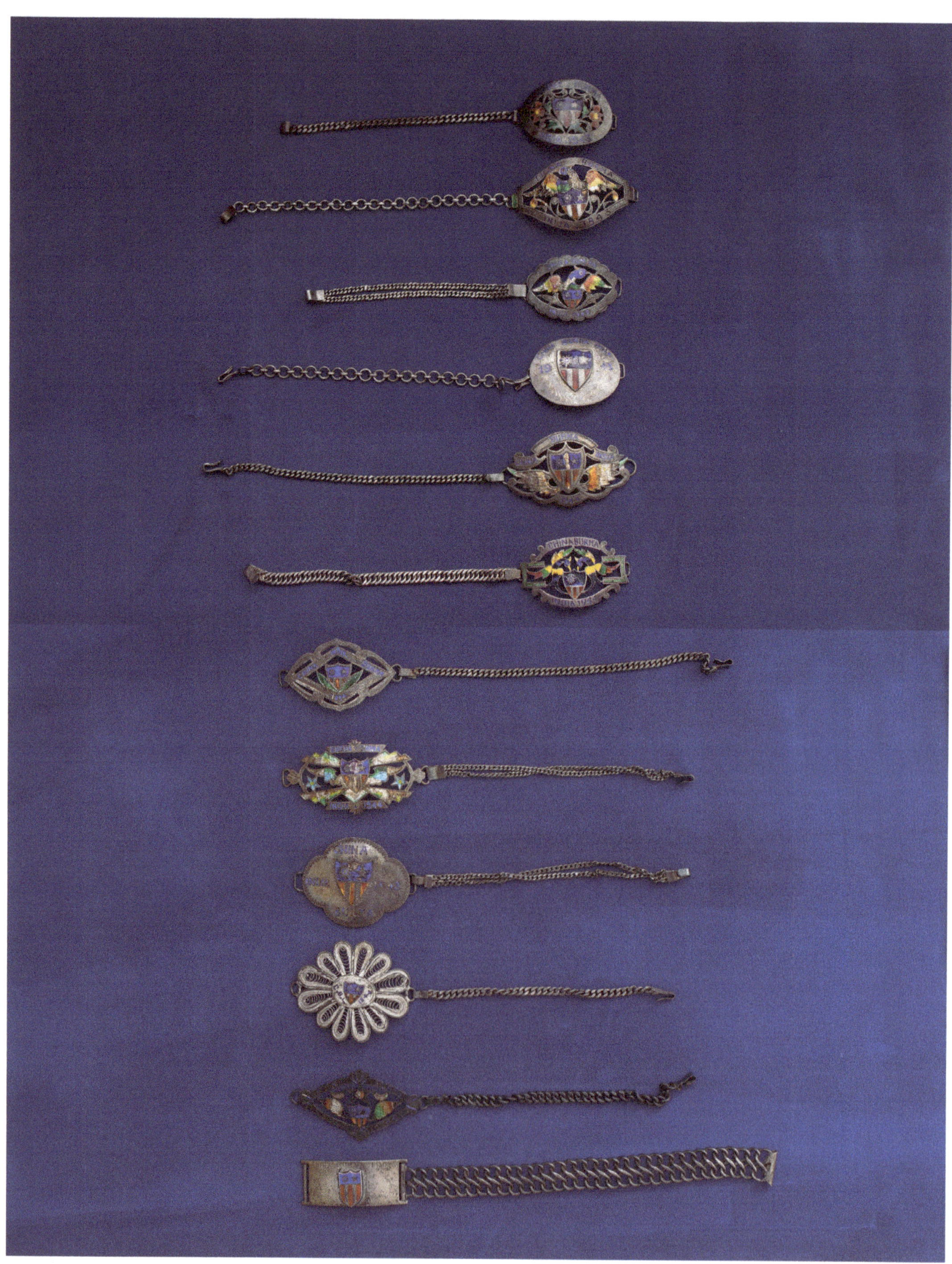

In-Service Eagles and Wings

This unique exhibit has such variety; it's hard to choose a favorite piece, which is why I buy all of them I can find!

The image of the eagle, or even his wing, is so impressive, it's not hard to see why these images stand for power and speed.

The most interesting pin, in my opinion, is a set of Army Air Corps wings and Navy wings. This had to have been a fascinating story for any father or mother to talk about—two sons who are flyers (maybe twins) or possibly father/son serving. This is the stuff movies are made of!

I'm sure you'll appreciate the simplicity and value of the rhinestone piece.

The detail on some is so clear, they are most likely hand carved. See if you can find the most unusual one. It reads: "Somewhere in France"!

It's hard to be sure what the ages are on most of these, but in my opinion, after decades of studying these pieces, I would say that 90 percent of the sixty-plus exhibited are from WWI. All others would be WWII. Sometimes you just have to take your best shot!

Due in large part to Captain Queisser and his in-service flag and the groundswell of patriotism it spawned, most of the pieces in circulation today are still from the world wars era. The Korean War, commonly referred to as the "Forgotten War," and the Vietnam War had far fewer items created, due to the low interest in patriotism at those times in our nation's history. I am honored to do my part in keeping patriotism alive and thriving in America. This collection is one small part of honoring our patriotic history. We stand in the shadow of great men, not the least of whom is Captain Queisser for his simple and powerful creation: the in-service flag.

Be sure not to miss the various war units that are indicated on hangers.

The metals used in most of this exhibit are gold, silver, pot metal, and mother-of-pearl.

You'll have to look carefully if you are interested in this exhibit. Although many pieces look similar, they have subtle variations in value, material, and even in the manufacturer.

Finally, everyone always asks about the MVPs of my collection: the Most Valuable Pin. In this exhibit the MVP pin on this page is the one embedded with diamonds and rubies. This pin cost eight hundred dollars, was·made by a jeweler, and is one of a kind. Another great story, apparently a wealthy family, in which a soldier possibly had it made for his mother.

In-Service Unique Pins

Among the most unique, the pins in this exhibit are as varied as the people who once wore them. I never get tired of looking through this collection.

Brass Infantry pin encircled with a wreath, which signifies a victory, crossed rifles with a gonfalon shape centered at the top with a blue in-service star. Very rare.

Although there are many of these metal pins with the gonfalon-shaped flag banner topped with the American bald eagle, this one is unique because it states specifically it is for "SWEETHEART OVERSEAS." Most commonly, the others simply were mass produced to say husband, brother, son, etc.

WWI rank pin signifying this piece belonged to a member of his family and was worn proudly in honor of his service. Sergeant rank insignia atop crossed rifles with "US" centered indicates this is a sergeant serving in the US Army Infantry.

Brass WWI Allied Forces pin with in-service flag signifying three family members in service. The waving banner across the top showcases the flags of Italy, America, France, Great Britain, and Romania over the in-service flag, with three blue stars hanging from two tiny chains. I've only found one of its kind in over forty years of collecting. Excellent condition.

Metal WWI Allied Forces pin. The straight banner across the top showcases the flags of Belgium, Great Britain, America, France, and Italy. The word "ARMY" between the banner and the in-service flag with one blue star signifies one family member in service. Excellent condition.

Brass WWI round button. "HERO LAND, NEW YORK," with shield representing the US flag. Very, very rare.

Brass WWI pin. Straight banner engraved with "SERVICE IN FRANCE." In-service flag hanging from two tiny chains, with one blue star signifying one family member in service. Very rare.

Manufactured metal top hat pin. "U.S. OVER THERE" stamped on top with an in-service flag with one blue star signifying one family member in service. Rare.

Brass WWI in-service pin. Unique in that it does not present the in-service flag. However, it is stamped with the words "A SON IN SERVICE" in the center flanked by victory wreath, beautifully draped across the bottom right corner with a red-white-and-blue stripe. Very unique. Very, very rare.

Metal WWII in-service pin. "USA" across the top, one blue star, and crossed rifles on the white center of the in-service flag. Excellent condition. Rare.

Metal WWII mass-produced diamond-shaped pin. This one is unique due to its subject matter. So few men or women served in the Army Air Corps in aeromechanics. Very rare.

Brass WWI US Marine Corps sergeant insignia topped with the in-service flag with one blue star. A family member to honor this US Marine would proudly wear this pin.

Metal WWI quartermaster pin. The uniqueness of this tiny pin is in the subject of the artwork on it. It showcases a field tent, which was a working warehouse of supplies needed by the troops while on the battlefield. It housed items such as food and personal care items—all such things needed to maintain health and well-being. Very good condition.

Plastic American flag and in-service pin. Two stars on the horizontal in-service flag suggest two family members serving. Although these mass-produced pins were inexpensive to make, by virtue of their age, about one hundred years now, they are very rare and hard to find in this condition.

Handmade from a reasonably good quality brass and crafted in the outline of the United States of America. This beloved pin, engraved with the words "MY SON IS SERVING" and "USA" across the top, speaks to the pride of the American family to have taken part in the effort to preserve freedom. This is the only one of its kind I personally have ever seen. Excellent condition.

Metal Liberty Bell with one blue star and "US" at the top. Among the smallest pins with a big message, embracing the things this family valued most: patriotism, liberty, and their dear family member in the service. Very rare.

WWI metal-forged Southern Cross of Honor–shaped pin depicting the Allied Forces that fought against Germany. Very rare. Only one of its kind I've ever come across in over forty years of collecting.

WWI metal pin. Unique in its design, "US" is cleverly crafted with the S inside the U and three in-service blue stars in the center white panel of a red-white-and-blue enamel background. Only one of its kind I've ever seen.

WWI metal pin. The words "IN SERVICE" engraved across blue enamel top bar; a simple heart hangs from a tiny chain. Such a small piece with a powerful message of love. Only one of its kind I've ever seen to date.

WWI paratrooper pin. The subject on this beautifully mastered pin commands a higher price than most. Pieces that depict the paratrooper are as rare as the paratroopers themselves. There just weren't that many men who chose to jump out of perfectly good airplanes back then. Those who did received a level of respect above that of the average soldier. Only one of its kind and quality I've ever seen.

WWI gold-plate pin. Only one of its kind I've ever seen. With an engraved US Navy man centered with red-white-and-blue ribbon behind him and a vertical in-service flag dangling from him. A single blue star depicts one member in the family serving. Very rare.

This beautifully crafted Coast Guard in-service pin truly has my heart. Besides there being fewer products to find on the subject of the Coast Guard, the pin boasts the US Coast Guard emblem carefully engraved at the top and a horizontal in-service flag with three blue stars, implying three family members in the service of the US Coast Guard. Rare branch of service, rare to have three people in service at the same time, and rare that this pin is so intricately engraved.

WWI manufactured pin. These inexpensively made pins rarely made it to the one hundredth birthday like this one has. Its uniqueness lies in its regional appeal. Clearly a Southern influence, with the words "I HAVE A BEAU IN THE SERVICE" stamped on a red-white-and-blue background.

WWI sterling silver and gold-plate pin. Original boxed pin. "US" painted with red-and-blue enamel, overlaid with a white enamel–painted bar with the word "SISTER" engraved in it. Hanging from a long, fragile chain is the Medical Corps insignia. Most likely a doctor in the service in this family, honoring sibling love.

WWI horizontal in-service pin with six family members serving at the same time. Imagine the heart of that mother! I've only come across two other pins of this kind with six stars. The current market value on this pin on eBay is valued at $250, and it grows higher every year. I clearly remember purchasing this pin twenty-five years ago and I paid $45 for it. This pin is a good example of long-term investment growth in pin collecting.

WWI silver-plate pin. Machine Gun Corps. With crossed machine guns, the initials "M" and "G" and an in-service shield with one blue star depicting one family member serving in the Machine Gun Corps.

WWI gold-plate pin. Machine Gun Corps. With crossed machine guns and a horizontal in-service flag with one blue star depicting one family member serving in the Machine Gun Corps.

Small brass pin. "USA MARINES" written across a red-and-blue enamel banner, American eagle with wings spread across the top, and a single white enamel star in the center. Rare.

WWII brass pin. Four branches of service emblems engraved on this very rare and beautiful pin honored all families and all branches of service that had one son in service of the US Armed Forces.

WWI brass pin. Engraved to honor one son in the service of the US Armed Forces. Unusual in that this in-service piece strayed far from the original design, with a red star atop a blue banner with the word "SON" on it and a larger "USA" across the bottom. Truly unique design.

In-Service Chain Pins

This exhibit is unique in that the pin is in two pieces, which attach in two different places on your lapel. The varying subject matter on each pin adds to the interest in this collection.

In-Service Medium to Large Pins

What makes this collection so unique is that these pins are larger than the rest of the pins in my collection. Ranging from WWI to WWII, these pins are mostly manufactured, but you will notice a few are clearly handmade as well. The sheer size of these pins shows the pride in the heart of the wearer. These people wanted all to know they proudly support the US soldier!

SON SERVING U.S. ARMY
BROTHER SERVING U.S. ARMY
BROTHER SERVING U.S. ARMY

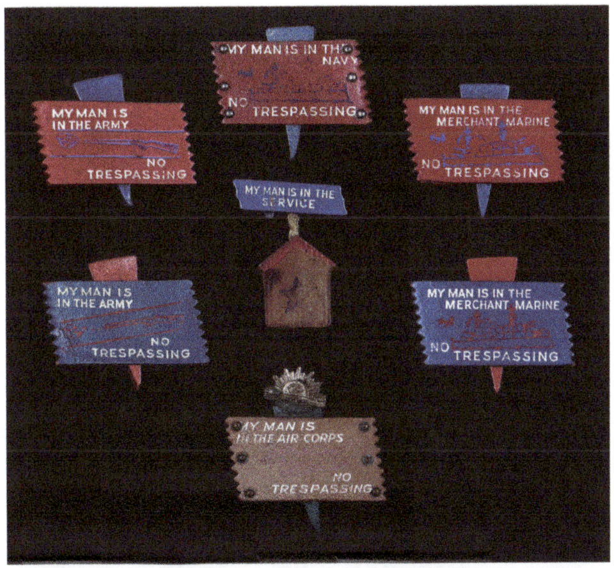
MY MAN IS IN THE NAVY
NO TRESPASSING
MY MAN IS IN THE ARMY
NO TRESPASSING
MY MAN IS IN THE MERCHANT MARINE
NO TRESPASSING
MY MAN IS IN THE SERVICE
MY MAN IS IN THE ARMY
NO TRESPASSING
MY MAN IS IN THE MERCHANT MARINE
NO TRESPASSING
MY MAN IS IN THE AIR CORPS
NO TRESPASSING

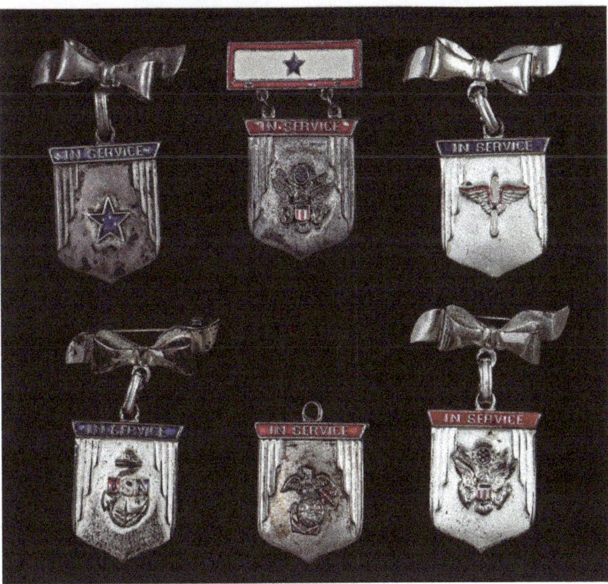
IN SERVICE
IN SERVICE
IN SERVICE
IN SERVICE
IN SERVICE
IN SERVICE

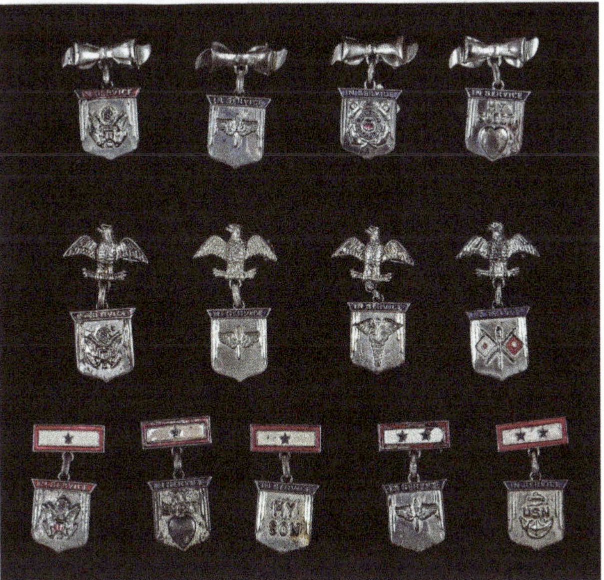
IN SERVICE
IN SERVICE
IN SERVICE
IN SERVICE
IN SERVICE
IN SERVICE
IN SERVICE
IN SERVICE
IN SERVICE
IN SERVICE
IN SERVICE
IN SERVICE
MY SON
USN

In-Service Military Pins

Tiny pins with a huge impact.

This exhibit clearly shows the growing interest in the in-service "movement." It started with a simple banner and is now growing to include a wide variety of items branded with the red, white, and blue.

About one hundred pins of the thousands that are in my collection will be showcased here; these are the tiniest in the collection.

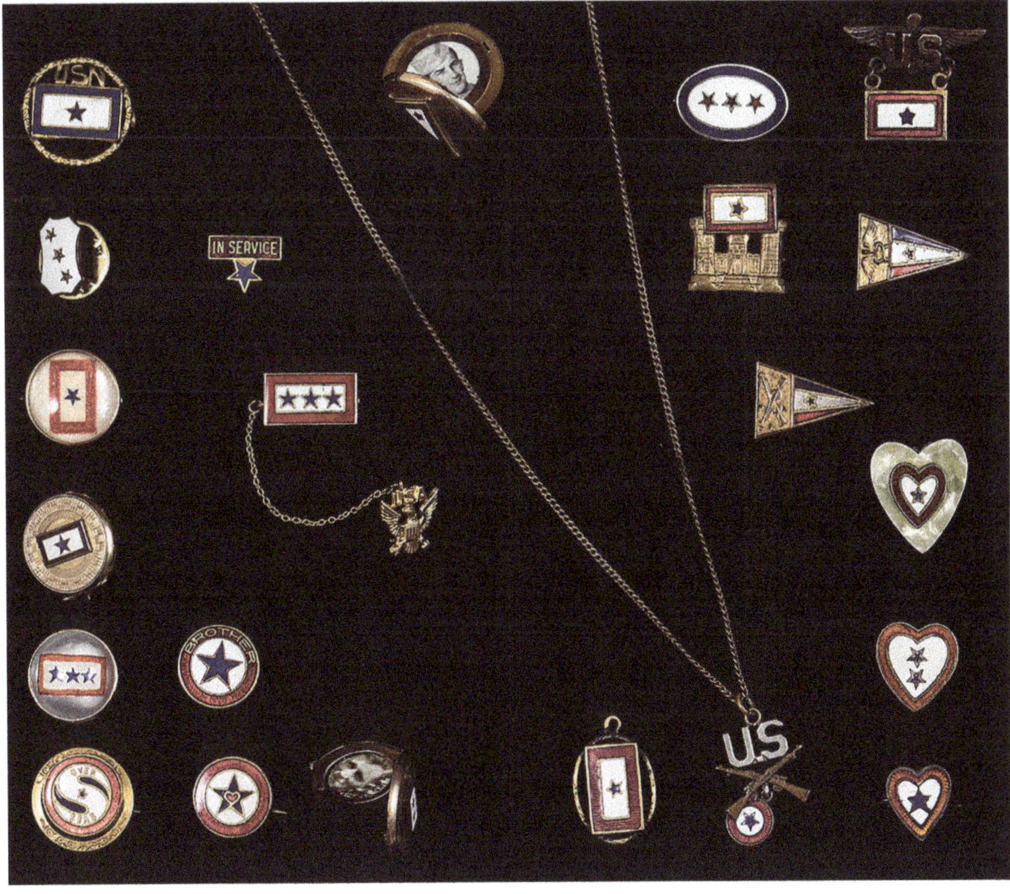

In-Service Military Rank Insignia Pins (Nonofficial)

This exhibit seemed strange to me, as people today typically don't wear these replicas of their soldier boy's rank. But in the world war era, they did. These strange pins would be worn by parents or loved ones in support of the soldier in their lives. Maybe it made them feel closer to him. Maybe it showed their pride in his achievements. Or maybe it was just their way to support the troops. Whatever the reason, it belonged only to them, and we would be wise to respect that.

In-Service Watch Fobs

The definition of a watch fob is a short chain or ribbon with an attached medallion or ornament. They were most often worn to display the service emblem. In early times, men did not wear a wristwatch as we do today. The fob was most often made of a chain, rope, or leather strap.

Though women wore the majority of in-service emblems, men also wanted to show their pride in sons or daughters serving in the Armed Forces.

WORLD
WAR
TRUE
TO
COLORS
SERVICE
IN
FIELD
1917

In-Service Record Books

These books can be considered a diary of a soldier's life.

As you will see in this exhibit, the in-service banner or the words "SERVICE" or "MY PART" are on the cover of each of these treasured books that detail a day in the life of a soldier. Even though many of them are never actually filled in, they still guide us through a process only a member of the military can truly know about. This is our chance to look a little deeper.

I never pass up a chance to open these books when I find them. They are most often empty, or if they have information in them, it's minimal. But then, you find one. A rare treasure such as the one in this collection: "My Part in the 2nd WORLD WAR," in which the author was prolific in his accounts, snapshots, and details, such as this one:

"Went to the USO dance and met Lena Horne; her secretary was better than she! (Oh boy!)"

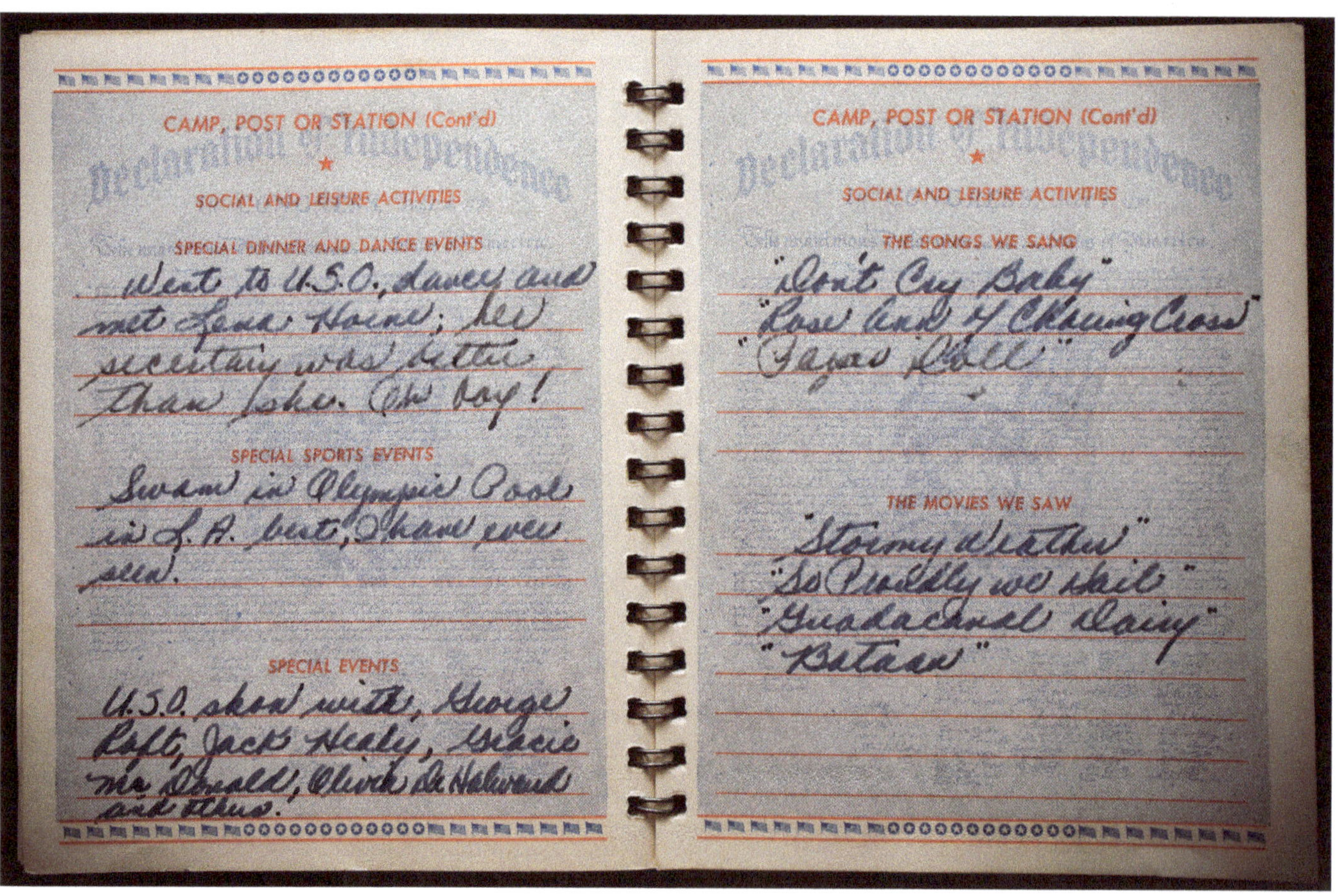

Circa 1914–19XX, this service-record book is leather bound and carefully preserved. The in-service banner carefully attached on the front of the book and the phrase "The Great World War" on the first page tell us this is a soldier's service-record diary from WWI. Please note, the date inscribed has no ending date because at the time this book was printed, no one knew when the war would actually end.

Printed by Pilgrim Press, and interestingly the copyright date is 1916.

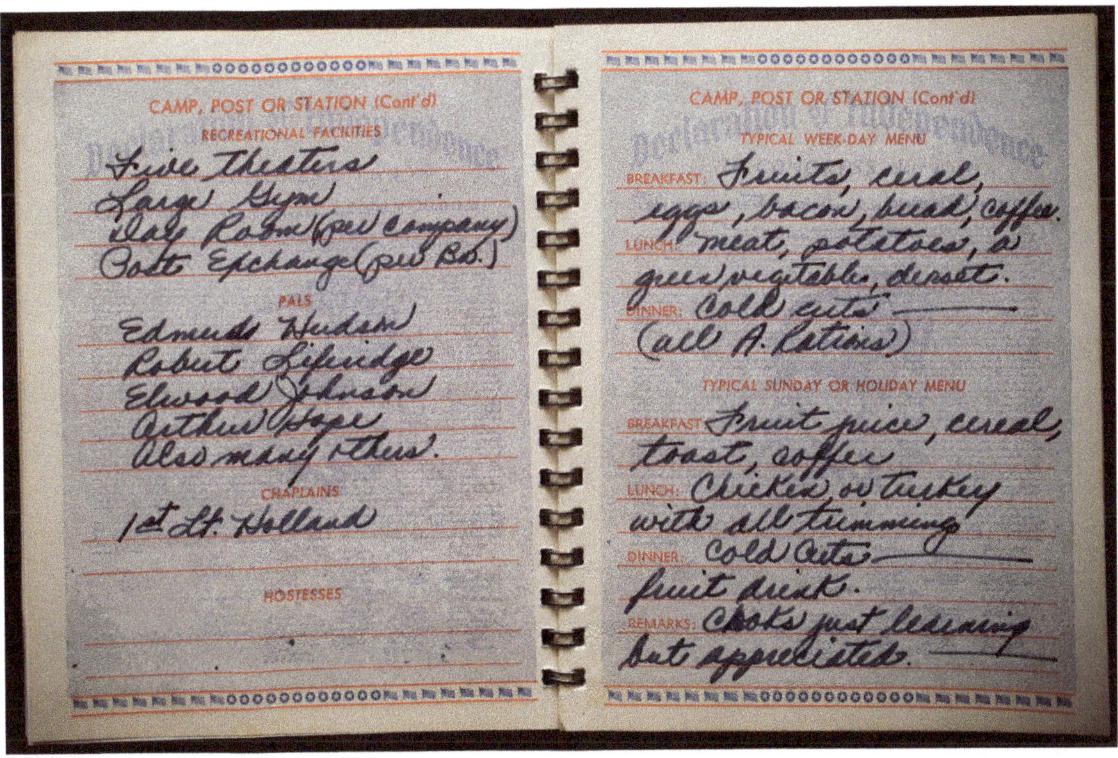

SERVICE
RECORD

The historic State of the Union–type speech by President Woodrow Wilson on April 2, 1917.

"TO SUCH A TASK WE CAN DEDICATE OUR LIVES AND OUR FORTUNES, EVERYTHING THAT WE ARE AND EVERYTHING THAT WE HAVE, WITH THE PRIDE OF THOSE WHO KNOW THAT THE DAY HAS COME WHEN AMERICA IS PRIVILEGED TO SPEND HER BLOOD AND HER MIGHT FOR THE PRINCIPLES THAT GAVE HER BIRTH AND HAPPINESS AND THE PEACE WHICH SHE HAS TREASURED. GOD HELPING HER, SHE CAN DO NO OTHER."

WOODROW WILSON'S WAR MESSAGE
APRIL 2ND, 1917

THE PURPOSE OF THIS RECORD

THIS book has been thoughtfully planned to enable you to keep and preserve the complete record of any relative or friend now with the armed forces of the United States. It is a book for which many have long felt a need, a book that will become increasingly valuable with age.

So many men who were engaged in the World War of 1917-18 have sorely regretted that they did not keep a record of their service with Uncle Sam — their affiliations and troop movements, where they went, and what they did, what they saw, when they returned, together with dates and other interesting data. Their wives and children also regret it.

"His Service Record" provides for that information in an organized manner — personal pre-war history, war service, photographs, clippings, places sent, friends and buddies, amusing incidents, interesting and exciting experiences; and also, space for citations, rank, service, branch and divisional insignia, and discharge papers. Space is likewise provided for a record of what happened in home and family circles, news of friends and important local events.

Much of this may be filled out at once from present knowledge, other happenings to be set down as they occur; also a record may be kept of prominent war figures, popular songs, war slogans, etc. Other pages may be completed as additional information is received. Maps of the United States and the World will enable relatives to keep a record of travel movement (when they are learned) and a pocket is provided in the back of the book for important letters received. Further data and vital information can be added when the MAN IN SERVICE returns home after his discharge.

"His Service Record," then, should become his personal property, for it will be complete — a record in black and white — at once an irreplaceable family heirloom — a treasured possession that will grow priceless in the years to come.

Page 4–7 They would place portraits and snapshots on these pages.

Page 8–9 Enlistment and training. Note that this is where they would write the forts or camps they trained at during the enlistment period of their service. There are many training camps throughout the country. First would be basic training; next assignment might be specialized training such as training in the use of modern-warfare equipment, like mortar, tank, or artillery training. Later, he might be sent further on to train in diverse environments preparing them for jungle, urban, or mountain warfare.

Page 10–11 Active service would more often mean Ship to Base in England and Australia or elsewhere in the Navy.

Page 12–13 Battles. Once an engagement grew into a "battle," it could require hundreds or thousands of others to join in. The Battle of the Bulge would be a great example of a battle. Never heard of it? Google it and find out how your freedom was preserved.

Page 14–15 Skirmishes and engagements could cover a couple of things known to happen in wartime. A "skirmish" could be a minor confrontation between a squad, normally eight to ten-plus men who went on patrol near enemy lines and were fired upon by one or more enemy combatants. When a skirmish would escalate, it would be considered an "engagement" that would require a call for support from other squad members or the platoon.

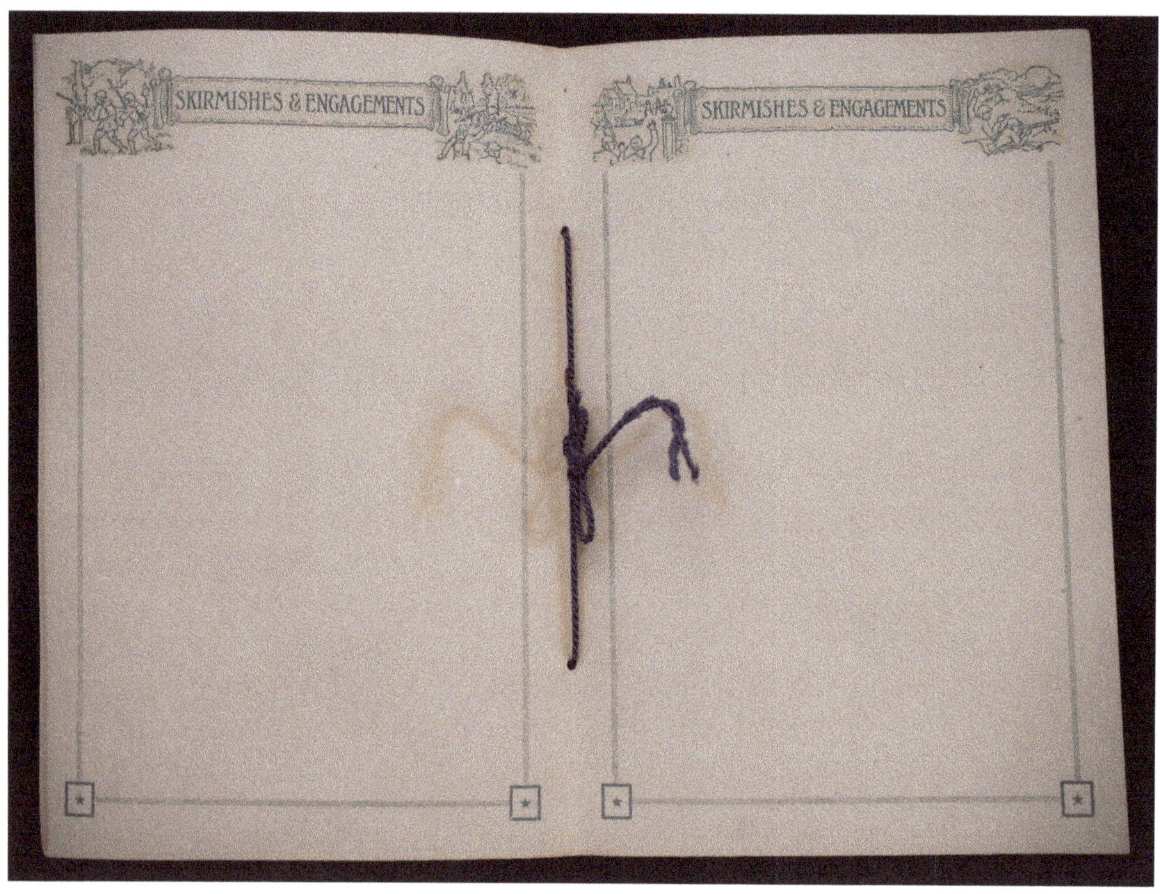

Page 16 Promotions and awards. When a soldier enters the Armed Forces, his first rank is "private," and he would carry this rank for six to twelve months then would receive a single stripe and be considered private first class. If he does well, he could achieve a second stripe and be considered a corporal. Continuing to do well, he could achieve a third stripe and be considered a sergeant. And on he could go to the highest rank an enlisted soldier could achieve, that of sergeant major. The term command sergeant major is a modern-day term.

Now we can discuss awards. The enlisted men or women start receiving merit awards in basic training. This would mean they temporarily wear the armband of a squad leader, meaning they are responsible for eight to ten soldiers. If they do well, they could receive Outstanding Trainer during Basic Training Battalion, a trophy generally presented upon graduation day in front of 250–500 soldiers and maybe thousands of guests.

The list of awards is very long, so I will cover only a few here:

Purple Heart Award—An enlisted soldier would receive this if he were wounded in combat.

Bronze Star—Heroic service and/or meritorious achievement during combat.

Silver Star—For gallantry in action against the enemy of the United States, the Silver Star is the third-highest personal decoration for valor in combat.

Distinguished Service Cross—For extreme gallantry and risk of life during combat, the Distinguished Service Cross is the second-highest personal decoration for actions of such a high degree, just short of the highest award . . .

Medal of Honor—The highest, oldest, and most continuously issued combat decoration in the history of the United States Armed Forces.

Reminiscences. This is the section in which to write whatever struck you as memorable if you wish to preserve your thoughts and insights for future generations.

Some of the most interesting things to military buffs would be personal accounts of military life.

Some of the most interesting points of interest for average Americans might be stories and accounts of personal interaction while on leave or sights in foreign countries such as the Tower of London, the Eiffel Tower, or the Vatican.

Still others might look for stories of friendships and the names and places pertinent to the account.

FOR GOD AND COUNTRY

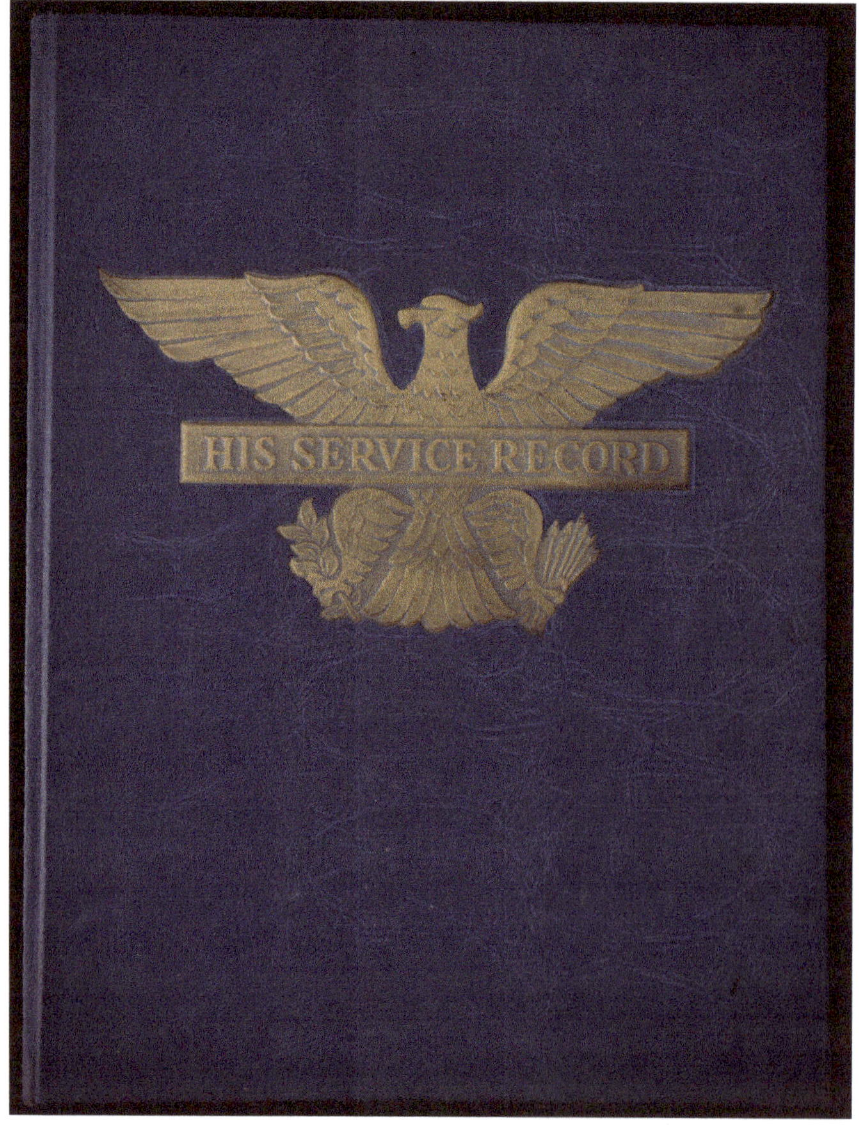
HIS SERVICE RECORD

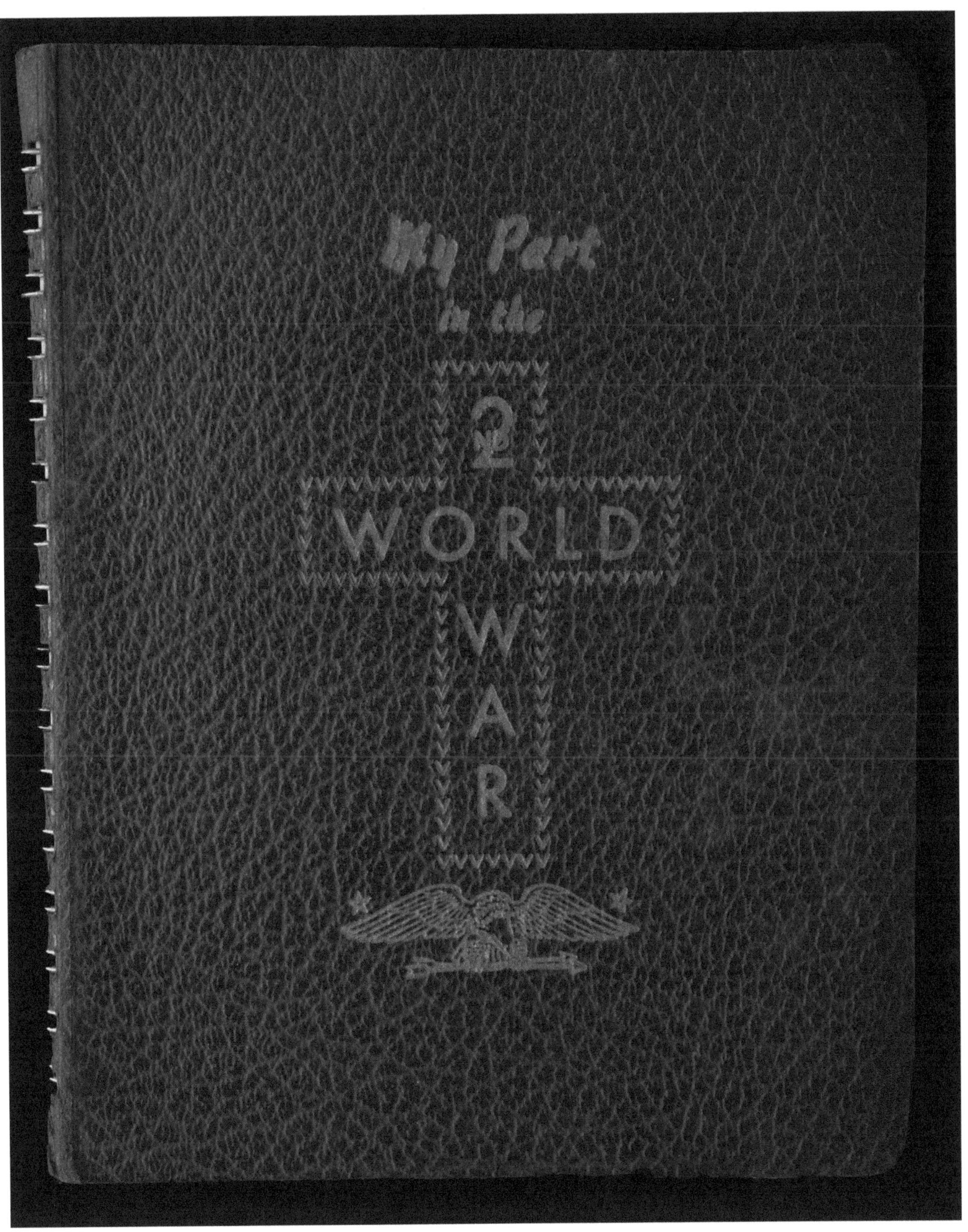
My Part
in the
2
WORLD
W
A
R

In-Service Vintage License Plates

History of the License Plate

New York was the first state to require residents to display identification tags on their automobiles. California soon followed, even requiring identification tags on bicycles and wheeled carts!

The first New York tags were of the "do-it-yourself" type. Residents were responsible for making their own and putting their initials and state name on them. These were often made of leather or rubber, or some people just painted the info right on the car.

As you can see, the use of homemade tags created problems. Once criminals caught on, they would simply create counterfeit tags. So in 1901 the state of New York realized that conformity was becoming necessary due to the growing volume of cheaper cars being bought by more people. (Thank you, Henry Ford!)

In 1903, the state of Massachusetts became the first to issue license plates. Early plates were made of iron coated with porcelain. (Can you imagine?) This practice didn't last, as the porcelain was too fragile.

In 1906 the state of Virginia designed the first stamped and embossed metal plates.

In 1915 the first Department of Motor Vehicles was established, and that led to all states being required to have license plates on all automobiles by 1918.

This worked well until 1943, when during WWII the rationing of metal was required for the war effort. There were no plates made of metal during the war, so the government started issuing replacement plates made of cardboard and stickers.

It was not until 1960 that the size of the license plate became uniform across the USA.

During WWII the in-service craze even permeated our love of automobiles; these are a few cardboard license plates that honor our boys in the service.

Red vertical plate with two Vs for victory at each of the top corners. "OUR SONS ARE IN SERVICE" and American flag with two stars at the bottom representing their two sons.

"THIS HOME IS LONELY WITHOUT OUR BOYS." Three stars and a sketch of three servicemen.

Red horizontal plate with a mother's prayer on it.

This horizontal plate actually depicts the in-service flag on it, with the words "SERVING OUR COUNTRY" on it.

Red horizontal plate has home-front sentiment on it with American flags, victory Vs, and stars. Patriotic pride at its finest.

In-Service WWI Variety of Items

United States of America entered into WWI when a British passenger ship called the *Lusitania* was sunk by a German submarine while at sea in 1915. This lit the anger toward Germany and soon America was at war. The ship had many American passengers on board at the time.

Those acts signaled President Woodrow Wilson to declare war on Germany. And a draft was started immediately to put a fighting force together.

In the beginning, the US Army did not have enough rifles to issue to men joining the service, but in short order, America dispatched General John Pershing to lead the Americans. Most American citizens were ill prepared for war and many resisted it, but to no avail; the motto was "We're in it to win it." The primary branches of service was the United States Army; thus, many of the in-service banners were used as posters and in-service pins were given as a result of WWI. The original was altered to fit a need, and that led to nearly every item manufactured from 1917 to 2017. One hundred years.

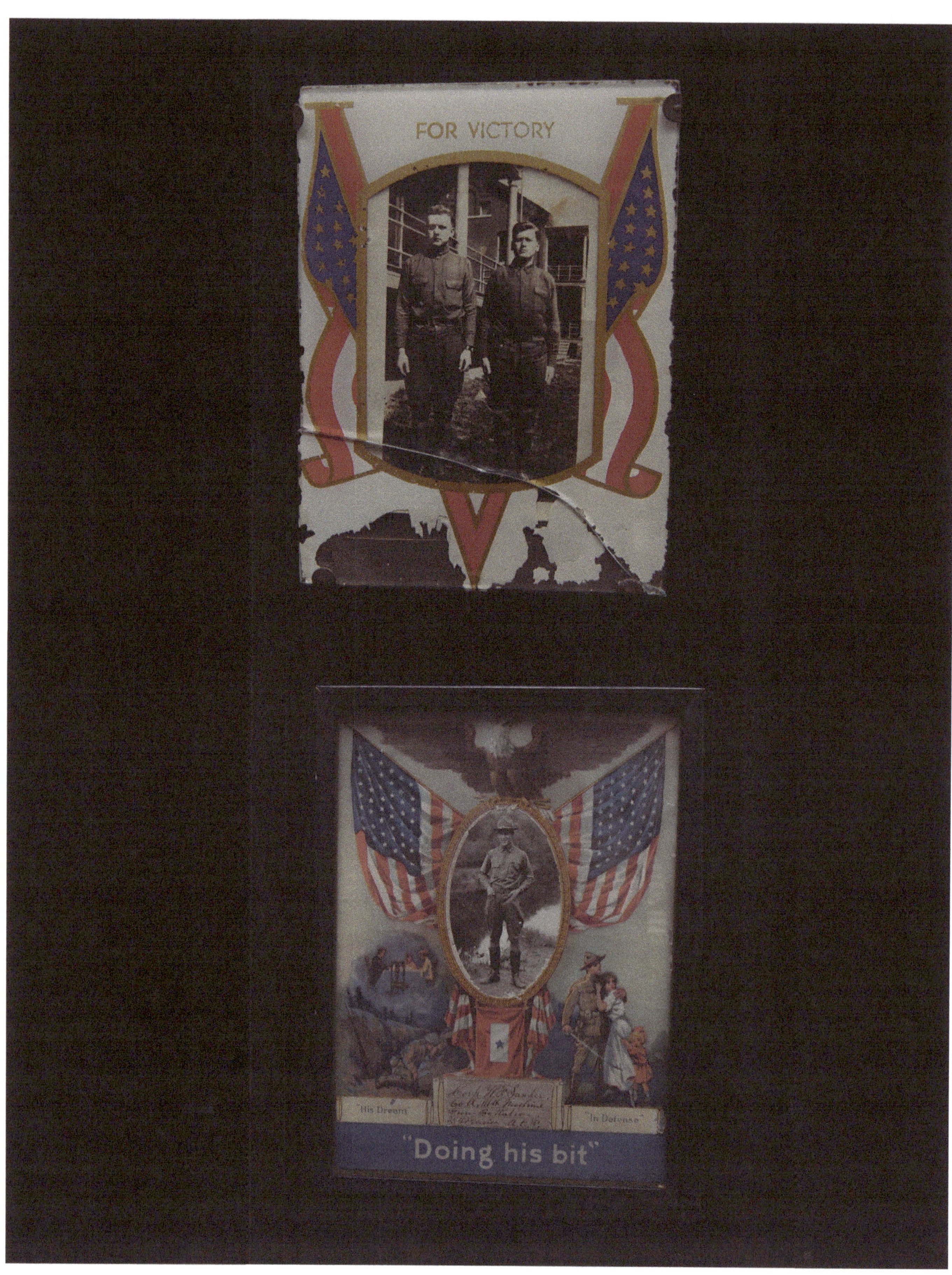
FOR VICTORY
"His Dream"
"In Defense"
"Doing his bit"

HOME OF A
SOLDIER

As you view this grouping, you will see bullets, bayonets, and crossed rifles in very unusual picture frames. One of the buyers of this book will spot their great-grandfather. As you view a variety of frames with stands to place on the nightstand, on top of the radio, or near a table by the front door, you will be letting everyone know someone in the family was in the US Army.

Soldiers'
and
Sailors'
Picture
Frames

Most of these are made of copper and brass.

ABOUT THE COLLECTION AND ITS ONGOING MISSION

The National Foundation of Patriotism was proud to begin unveiling portions of the Sweetheart Jewelry Collection exhibit in 2017-2018. The exhibit is the private collection of Nicholas D. Snider and features pieces from one of the world's largest collections of its kind. Its history spans from Civil War era to the Vietnam era with a few pieces up to Desert Storm at this time.

The Sweetheart Jewelry Collection is a traveling exhibit; its "road name" is Rescuing a Piece of Romantic History and is offered, on loan, to museums, government buildings, corporate headquarters, and colleges. We have had an exhibit at Hartsfield-Jackson International Airport in Atlanta, Georgia, for the past nine years and are currently undergoing a refreshing redesign and expansion to be completed late 2020-2021.

THE HISTORY OF MILITARY SWEETHEART JEWELRY AND COLLECTIBLES

What is it? It is an important part of American history! Each piece represents the love of a soldier and the women in his life. Mother, wife, sweetheart, sister. The exhibits feature pins, rings, bracelets, banners, pennants, pillowcases, patches, compacts, and more.

Who collected it? This book represents pieces from the private collection of Nicholas D. Snider. The entire collection to date spans to over ten thousand pieces. Nick recognized the patriotic importance of this exhibit and included it in the National Foundation of Patriotism exhibits. He has written two books on the subject and collaborated on a third.

Where did it come from? Nick traveled the world researching and collecting facts, artifacts, personal stories, letters, poetry, and pictures that round out the entire story of this unique compilation.

When was it made? The oldest pieces date to the Civil War era; the newest are from Vietnam to Desert Storm.

Why will people like it? Those who love military history, romantic memorabilia, and American soldiers and their sweethearts appreciate the collection—as well as all red-blooded American patriots!

ABOUT THE AUTHOR

Nicholas (Nick) D. Snider

Retired Senior Vice President, United Parcel Service (UPS)

Philanthropist, Author, Collector, Patriot

Nick Snider's life has always been centered on service. He served in the US Army as a commissioned officer, followed by a thirty-three-year career with United Parcel Service (UPS). Snider was actively involved in numerous UPS community projects and was instrumental in building and developing its worldwide volunteer program. He was awarded the first national UPS Corporate Community Service Award, now given annually. He is an active supporter of the USO and currently serves on the Georgia USO Board of Directors, as well as many others (see below). A commissioned officer of the United States Army and a 1965 graduate of Officer Candidate School, he is a lifetime collector of patriotic jewelry and collectibles, of which he has acquired one of the world's largest collections. He has authored two books on patriotic collecting (1995 and 1996) and collaborated on a third in 2000. For many years, he has dedicated his life to creating the National Museum of Patriotism in Atlanta, which opened on July 4, 2004. The museum's mission is to promote the history of patriotism, to encourage people to examine what patriotism means to them, and to educate students and promote civic participation.

More recently, Nick has guided the National Foundation of Patriotism in partnership with many other organizations like the Medal of Honor Society and Foundation, as well as Library of Congress projects and many other service organizations. Through the National Foundation of Patriotism, Nick focuses his efforts on reaching all generations with a message of positive American patriotism through the foundation's website, social media, causes, and events.

Nick Snider is available for interviews as a leading authority on patriotism, and motivational speaker, for your next event.

Our Patriotic Goal

It is our goal to inspire you to remember the definition of patriotism, share it with others, and get involved with family, colleagues, and friends in community activities and civic responsibilities. We wish to inspire you to help us expand our base and reach one million followers in 2019. We have over a quarter million following us already. We need your momentum. If each one of you would invite three people to do three things, we can reach our goal!

1. Like us on Facebook.

2. Share our posts.

3. Donate to help us continue expanding our reach.

Honors and Awards

- Recipient of the Citizen of the Year Award, West Point Society (Georgia Chapter).
- Recipient of the SAR Distinguished Patriotic Leadership Award, National Sons of the American Revolution.
- Recipient of the DAR Medal of Honor, National Daughters of the American Revolution.
- Carried the Olympic Torch in the Atlanta Centennial Olympic Games in 1996.
- Led the development and deployment of the DIAD (Delivery Information Acquisition Device) system and spearheaded its conversion to all UPS drivers.
- Recipient of the USO Patriot Award.

Accolades and Service

- Member of the Board of Directors, Balance-Certified Golf Co.
- Member of the Board of Directors, United Service Organization Inc. (USOGA).
- Chairman and Founder of the National Foundation of Patriotism (est. 1996 Atlanta, Georgia).
- Retired Vice President 1998 United Parcel Service, Inc. Employed thirty-three years.
- Managed the company's largest handheld computer device ever deployed worldwide in 1991.
- Built the corporation's volunteer program for worldwide application.
- Nick is one of five siblings (four brothers and one sister) who served in the US Army. He went in as an enlisted man and later attended Officer Candidate School, Fort Benning, Georgia. Received rank of first lieutenant. Nick served in Germany as well as USA.
- Entrepreneur of the Year—Club E, College Park (Atlanta), Georgia.
- Recipient of the first United Parcel Service "Volunteer of the Year" award for his leadership in the successful completion of a three-year assignment as an "on-loan" executive to the Atlanta Project guided by former President Jimmy Carter.

OTHER BOOKS BY NICHOLAS D. SNIDER

A MESSAGE TO COLLECTORS

Collectors are Protectors!

We invest in America's history. We rescue and preserve some of the most amazing pieces of the fabric of American culture.

A major part of my adult life has been spent in thrift shops, military surplus stores, flea markets, and military trade shows just mining the treasures of our military history. I have amassed one of the largest collections of military sweetheart jewelry and collectibles in the world.

At this stage of my collector life, I wish to pass along a few tips to the next generation of collectors—in particular, the four main factors of collecting:

Research—Once you choose your subject, it is imperative you become very specific when you start your research. Beware: it's hard to keep your focus! I started with wing pins and now have over ten thousand pieces in about fifty categories.

Network—Find your tribe! This will prove to be the most enjoyable and fulfilling part of your collector's experience—trading, sharing, selling, and buying. I found my person at military trade shows, antique and collectible shows, flea markets, estate sales, and garage sales and even traveled to four different countries: Canada, France, England, and Australia.

Pricing—One of the most challenging aspects of collecting is making the determination of what to pay. Sometimes there is just no way around good old hard work and determination; in this case, comparison shopping is the best way to determine what the value of your piece truly is. But consider this: dealers/sellers often have to include their overhead into the cost of the item; likewise, you may want to track your expenses in pursuit of your treasure.

What I learned from the progression of collecting over the years—from the Sears catalog (circa 1940s) to eBay, my, have times changed! I started in the 1980s before the internet existed as we know it. The only place I could find my wing pins was at military shows, primarily. Now with the internet, the research is vast, but it does have its down side—namely, you lose the personal connection with dealers and sellers you come to know and trust. Another challenge is there is no personal interchange or haggling; now we have blind bidding on the computer. Sitting at your desk blind bidding cannot compare to the experience and excitement of going on the hunt for the next treasured piece. So I would suggest you try to make human connections whenever you can and watch out for the last-second bid!

PLEDGE OF ALLEGIANCE

(Stand at attention, right hand over heart, facing the flag.)

I Pledge Allegiance to the flag of the United States of America, and to the Republic, for which it stands, one nation under God, indivisible, with Liberty and Justice for all.

NATIONAL ANTHEM

(Stand at attention, right hand over heart, facing the flag, and sing.)

Oh, say, can you see
By the dawn's early light
What so proudly we hailed
At the twilight's last gleaming?

Whose broad stripes and bright stars
Through the perilous fight
O'er the ramparts we watched
Were so gallantly streaming.

And the rockets red glare,
The bombs bursting in air,
Gave proof through the night
That our flag was still there.
(chorus)
Oh, say, does that star-spangled
Banner yet wave
O'er the land of the free
And the home of the brave?

YOUR IN-SERVICE FLAG!

(Cut out, affix the stars, and hang it with pride.)

Patriotism matters. I wanted to give families an opportunity to teach the next generation what patriotism means to you. The following page is a replica of an in-service flag with extra stars.

Please use this page to teach patriotic values. Honor a soldier or soldiers in your life by affixing additional stars for each service member you know. We started you off with two additional stars.

Please visit the National Foundation of Patriotism website at www.foundationof patriotism.org and join us on all our social media channels. Our blog has topics that make it easy to start these conversations with young people; topics like "patriotism at home" and "patriotism around the dinner table" are especially useful to spark your creativity and give you a place to begin. God bless you, and may God continue to bless America!

Conversation Starter:

1. Tell what patriotism means to you.

2. Tell how you practice patriotism.

    a. Honor patriotic holidays.

    b. Fly the US flag on your house.

    c. Participate in parades.

3. Invite them to participate with you.

Major Patriotic Days:

- Memorial Day, Last Monday in May

- Flag Day, June 14

- Independence Day, July 4

- Patriot Day, September 11

- Veterans Day, November 11

www.ingramcontent.com/pod-product-compliance
Lightning Source LLC
Chambersburg PA
CBHW042057030726
47602CB00003B/53

9 781732 342729